The Life Cycle of a

SWALLOW

John Williams

Illustrated by
Jackie Harland

Reading Consultant:
Diana Bentley

The Bookwright Press
New York · 1989

Life Cycles

First published in the
United States in 1989 by
The Bookwright Press
387 Park Avenue South
New York, NY 10016

First published in 1988 by
Wayland (Publishers) Limited
61 Western Road, Hove
East Sussex, BN3 1JD, England

Library of Congress Cataloging-in-Publication Data
Williams, John
  The life cycle of a swallow/John Williams: illustrated by
  Jackie Harland; reading consultant, Diana Bentley,
      p. cm.—(Life cycles)
  Bibliography: p.
  Includes index.
  Summary: Describes the physical characteristics,
  habits, life cycle, and habitats of the graceful
  migratory bird the swallow.
  ISBN 0-531-18258-4
  1. Swallows—Juvenile literature. (1. Swallows.) I. Harland.
  Jackie, ill.   II. Title.   III. Series.
  Ql.696.P247W54 1989   88-10260
  598.8 13-dc19   CIP
                                                     AC

Typeset in the UK by DP Press Limited, Sevenoaks, Kent
Printed by Casterman S.A., Belgium

Notes for parents and teachers
Each title in this series has been specially written and
designed as a first natural history book for young readers.
For less able readers there are introductory captions,
while the more detailed text explains each illustration.

Contents

All the words that are
in **bold** are explained in
the glossary on page 31.

These birds are called swallows.

Look at these beautiful birds. They are called swallows. They swoop and dive in the air. They can fly for very long distances with their strong, pointed wings. Their feathers are a deep blue-black color and they have **forked** tails that help them change direction quickly in the air.

6

Swallows in the spring.

At the end of each summer, swallows leave their nests and fly to a warmer **climate**. This flight is called a **migration**. Swallows do not like the cold winters. But when it is spring, they will return to build new nests for their young.

A male and female swallow build a nest.

Swallows like to live where there is lots of space. They do not like noisy towns. A male and female swallow will build their nest in a quiet place in the country. They make their nest out of mud and straw. It takes about eight days to build a nest.

8

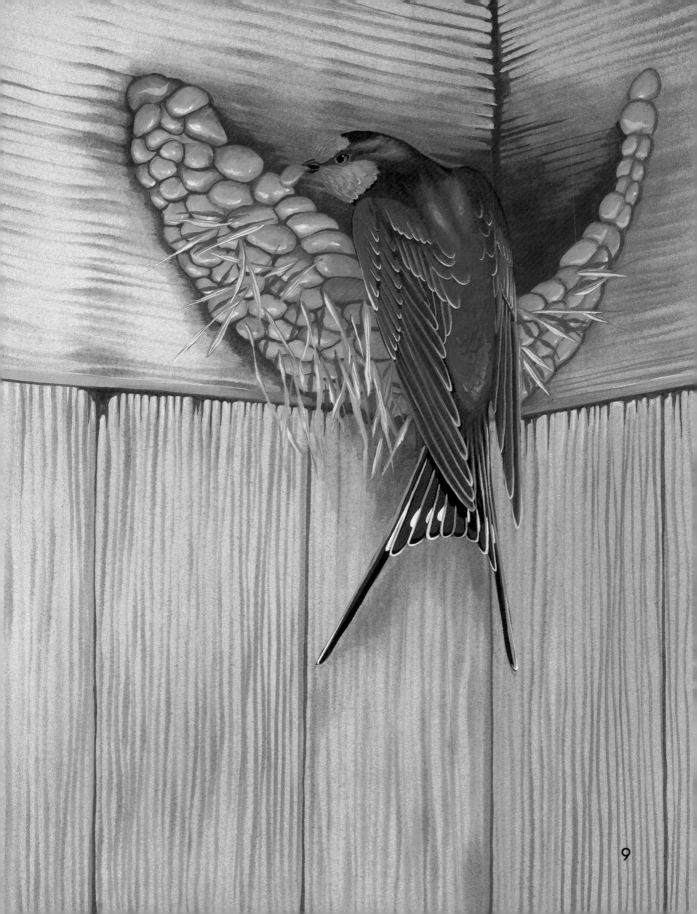

The male swallow **mates** with the female.

Before the female swallow can lay her eggs, the male must mate with her. He puts a liquid inside her called **sperm**. The sperm joins with the eggs inside the female swallow. This is called **fertilization**. The eggshells can now begin to form to protect the baby bird that will grow inside each egg.

The female swallow lays her eggs.

The female swallow lays her eggs from one to three days after mating with the male. She can lay up to six eggs and she often lays two or three **clutches**. The eggs must be kept warm, so the mother and father take turns covering them with their bodies.

13

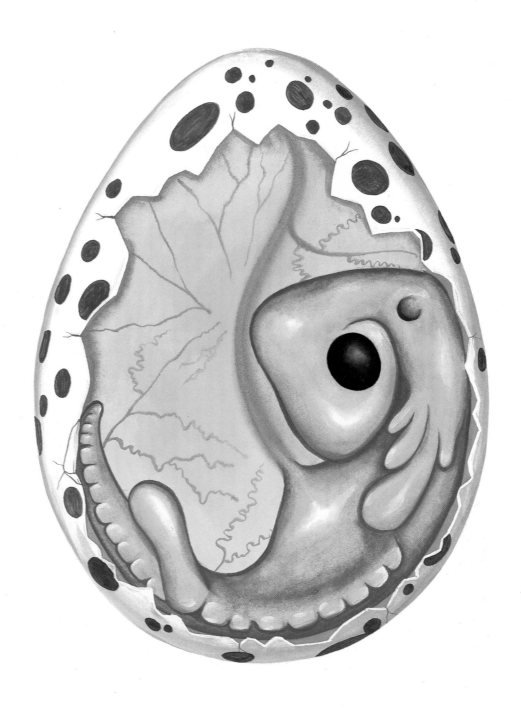

The young swallows grow inside the eggs.

Inside the egg, the young bird begins to grow. When the bird is inside the egg it is called an **embryo**. All the other parts of the egg are used up as food for the growing bird.

The mother and father look after the eggs.

As the young birds grow inside the eggs, the food is used up. The mother and father birds still look after the eggs. They take turns catching food for each other. Swallows eat flying insects, which they catch as they fly.

The young swallows come out of their eggs.

About fifteen days after the eggs are laid, the young birds begin to **hatch**. When they are first born, the baby birds have a thin layer of pale gray **down** on their backs. They have no feathers, so their parents have to keep them warm with their bodies and look after them.

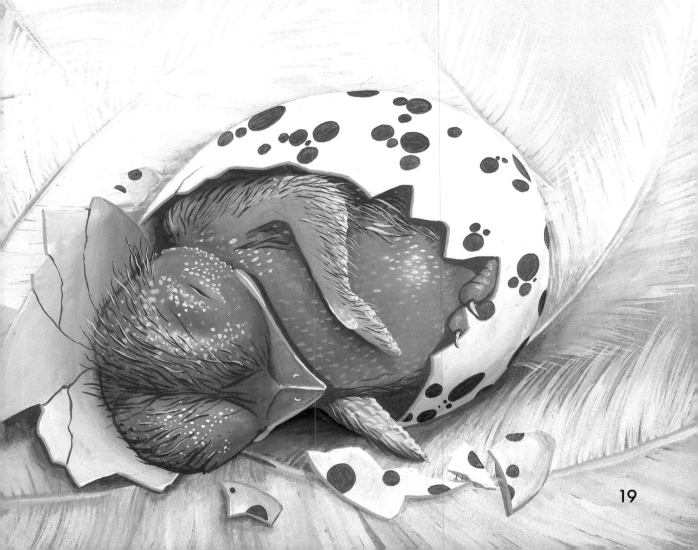

The mother and father feed their young.

The young swallows need to be fed right away. The parent birds must catch many flying insects to feed their babies and themselves. In the summer, you can see swallows swooping and chasing after insects as they fly.

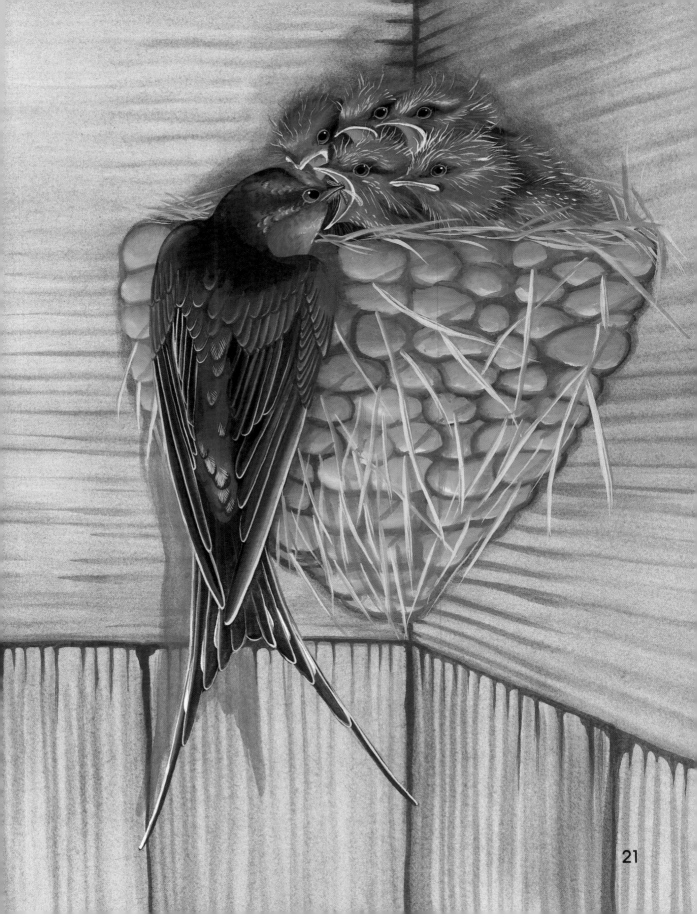

The young swallows are ready to fly.

About three weeks have passed. The young birds have grown feathers. They will soon be able to fly and catch their own food. They have been well fed and looked after by their parents. They are ready to leave the nest.

The young swallows leave the nest.

When the young swallows leave the nest, their mother and father keep on feeding them. But, instead of bringing food to the nest, they feed them while they are flying or **perching**. For the first few days the young swallows come back to the nest to sleep.

25

Full-grown swallows.

At the end of the summer, the swallows fly away in large **flocks** to spend the winter in a warmer place. Next spring, the young swallows will return to look for quiet places to build their own nests. What do you think will happen then?

Looking at birds.

There are many different kinds of birds that you can watch. In large towns and cities, you can see pigeons, sparrows and starlings. In the country, look for swallows, swifts and magpies.

If you find a bird's nest, look inside for eggs but do not touch them or the nest. It is very important not to disturb the nest as that might frighten the parent birds and make them leave the nest.

The life cycle of a swallow.

How many stages of the life cycle can you remember?

Glossary

Climate The weather conditions of a country or area.

Clutches Groups of eggs. A swallow can lay up to three clutches during the spring.

Down A soft, fluffy covering that baby birds are often born with, before they grow real, full sized feathers.

Embryo The word for a young bird or animal before it is born.

Fertilization The moment when the sperm from the male joins the eggs of the female so as to cause a new animal to develop.

Flocks Groups of birds or animals that feed or travel together.

Forked Divided into two points to form a v-shape.

Hatch To break out of an egg.

Mate To join together as male and female, to produce young. In mating, the female's eggs are fertilized by the male sperm.

Migration A journey from one country or area to another, especially when the seasons change.

Perching Alighting or resting upon a narrow place such as a branch or twig.

Sperm A liquid from the male that fertilizes the female's eggs.

Finding out more

Here are some books to read to find out more about swallows and other birds.

A First Look at Birds by Millicent E. Selsam and Joyce Hunt. (Walker & Co., 1973)

A First Look at Birds' Nests by Millicent E. Selsam. (Walker & Co., 1984)

The Bird Book by Laura Storms. (Lerner Publications, 1982)

Birds Do the Strangest Things by Leonora and Arthur Hornblow. (Random House, 1965)

Index